Pieces of Perspective

Written by

Chantel K. Demolle

Pieces of Perspective

Copyright © 2015 by Chantel K. Demolle

All rights reserved. This book or any portion thereof may not be reproduced or used in any manner whatsoever without the express written permission of the publisher except for the use of brief quotations in a book review or scholarly journal.

First Printing: 2015

ISBN 978-0-692-48641-2

Published by Chantel K. Demolle, Incorporated.

www.chanteldemolle.com

TABLE OF CONTENTS

I. DEDICATION
II. REDEMPTION
III. LOVE
IV. FREEDOM
V. TEARS
VI. PURPOSE
VII. PERSEVERANCE
VIII. FEAR
IX. IDENTITY
X. FAITH
XI. BEAUTY
XII. COURAGE
XIII. CONTENTMENT
XIV. DISCIPLINE
XV. FORGIVENESS
XVI. MIRACLES
XVII. REPUTATION
XVIII. JOY
XIX. TIMING
XX. GRATITUDE
XXI. JUSTICE
XXII. PROLOGUE

Dedication

This book is written for my son, Justice. It was created to be a lifetime of dedication and a life-long guide for him. Its words are my take on certain aspects of life and my advice on particular matters of the heart that will be forever available to him. And to world.

-Love Always-

"People, even more than things, have to be restored, renewed, revived, reclaimed, and redeemed; never throw out anyone."

- Audrey Hepburn

Redemption

Stars fall, stars shoot, stars strategically align
Guiding spotlights for the lost who seek to find
Amidst thick wilderness and deep darkness, stars shine
Sparks of hope, they lend comfort to the hopeless mind

Soon, the day will break with a welcomed appearance
Long nights are forgotten by this daily forgiveness
Rays of purple and orange stain the sky with their kiss
A new horizon unfolds with promises of bliss

The past is held captive in yesterday's grasp
Light years away floats the decaying mass
A new day springs forth, boasting lively contrasts
Renewed outlooks give birth to purposeful forecasts.

"Who, being loved, is poor?"

-Oscar Wilde

Love

A love deferred can haunt you, following you around

Crowded rooms, still lack of fulfillment abound

Relationships begin and end, enjoyable memories there-in

Never quite reaching the ungraspable within

Likened to passionate destiny, you'll know when it's come

Similar to gifting and purpose for a life well done

Until the inexplicably intangible is won

You'll feel consistently distant until you find that one

Not quite a fish out of water or a tree planted in sand

Not sure of the true fit but confident you'll know its hand

Never had it before and can't describe how it looks

Yet when it comes it's undeniable and can't be mistook

"My definition of a free society is a society where it is safe to be unpopular."

-Adlai Stevenson

Freedom

Everything used to matter before
How I did my hair and what I wore
What people thought of me was hard to ignore
Whatever I possessed, I always envied more

Didn't want to fit in yet afraid to stand out
Self-Identity defined by whatever's about
Vulnerable to my surroundings, I walked in self-doubt
Who was I to explore such an unchartered route?

After series of failures and multiple heartbreaks
Heavy burdens that seem like more than you can take
You break free from life's confines and finally escape
You've now found yourself and begin to take shape

Your life's experiences created you and not their perceptions
Liberty is had when you denounce their reactions
Abandoning others' opinions to be the exception
Will be your biggest fight and greatest life lesson

"Unless you have been very, very lucky, you have undoubtedly experienced events in your life that have made you cry. So unless you have been very, very lucky, you know that a good, long session of weeping can often make you feel better, even if your circumstances have not changed one bit."

-Lemony Snicket

Tears

Tears are shed for countless reasons

Joy or pain, reflective of the season

An overwhelming display of emotion, they fall

A personal prayer when there's no one to call

What words can't express, they clearly cry out

What your mouth can't say, they shamelessly shout

When your heart is touched in ways that you've never known

Your tears signal the harvest of what's been sown

Don't shy away from such beautiful displays

Your soul's interpretation of what you can't convey

There is something inside that's beyond explanation

Let your tears be response to your inner conversation

"The purpose of life is not to be happy. It is to be useful, to be honorable, to be compassionate, to have it make some difference that you have lived and lived well."

-Ralph Waldo Emerson

Purpose

Everything happens for a reason—such a cliché
Even the horrible things?—that's the biggest debate
Why do I have to go through this when others don't?
What makes me have to deal with what others won't?

How will this relate to my overall growth?
It's bad, yet good for me? How can it be both?
While others appear to be enjoying life
Why am I so consumed with what's wrong and what's right?

I want to be care-free with no conviction or thought
Yet everything is always something to be taught
I've tried to hide from all that life has to show me
But it won't loose me from the grips of destiny

Good, bad, and ugly—-they all hold meaning
Customized to the individual for one-on-one teaching
And yes, it appears, it's all for a reason
Don't miss the climate of life for a mere season

"Most of the important things in the world have been accomplished by people who have kept on trying when there seemed to be no help at all."

-Dale Carnegie

Perseverance

I almost fainted, so tired from constantly going

I've given all that I have and I'm still owing

The sun's rays are relentless and so is this journey

What I thought was mine maybe just isn't for me

My feet hurt from trails that lack paved comfort

Land as developed as a barren desert

I've lost all confidence that I'm headed the right way

No signs, no water, just the setting of new days

My strength has failed me and I'm not who I was

Trial after trial, seemingly just cause

I persevere only because I've abandoned all else

This journey has become the definition of myself

Whatever reason I first started on this winding road

I've traveled too far to return to old

I've travailed too long to consider it vanity

I will absolutely press on for what I am sure to see

"We are more often frightened than hurt; and we suffer more from imagination than from reality."

-Seneca

Fear

Fear is a merely a word created for control

It prevents the eye from having all it beholds

It stops the pursuer right in her tracks

It mocks his conceived plan of attack

Fear keeps you where it wants you, right under its thumb

A life born for living is unnaturally numb

A world set to conquer is overwhelmingly massive

A strong will sits back, cowardly passive

Fear is no longer a word, but the enemy of state

It alters the state of your being and state of your fate

It boxes in dreams and pokes fun at fantasy

It laughs at the idea of changing legacy

Fear is pervasive if you allow it to be

Fear is paralyzing, cutting at the knee

Fear is paradoxical, existing only in thought

Fear is merely a word until you have fought

"You have to leave the city of your comfort and go into the wilderness of your intuition. What you'll discover will be wonderful. What you'll discover is yourself."

-Alan Alda

Identity

A successful relationship, what does that mean?

I'm hot, you're cold, together something in between?

Meeting in the middle because compromise is key?

Or opposites attract is how it should be?

My father did this and my mother said that

I grew up hearing this so that makes it fact

My family has always done it this way

If you're going to be with me, it's that or highway

Who still does that anymore, it's so played out?

Your old-fashioned ways have since timed out

My favorite song explained how, and that's how I know

They did it this way on that new TV show

How do you define what it is you believe?

Is your life led by precepts that were preconceived?

Where did you learn that which you know?

Are your habits mere replicas of how they said it should go?

"Faith is not simply a patience which passively suffers until the storm is past. Rather, it is a spirit that bears things...with blazing serene hope."

-Corazon Aquino

Faith

Never be consumed by what you can't change

Full of worry, yet unable to rearrange

Those things in your life beyond your control

At what point is it better to just let go?

Despite your sundress, raindrops fall from the sky

After your loyalty, you're still told a lie

Even when you fight in all earnestness

You could still lose if the battle is fixed

What then, do you do when this happens to you?

Do you vow to give up and never pursue?

Will you resent all the times you've ever tried?

Accepting the notion that you'll live dissatisfied?

Life, unfortunately, is indeed a box of chocolates

A bite as fervent as before, but who knows what you'll get

You are still responsible to attack it the same

Never losing hope, because it's anyone's game

"Beauty can be consoling, disturbing, sacred, profane; it can be exhilarating, appealing, inspiring, chilling. It can affect us in an unlimited variety of ways. Yet it is never viewed with indifference: beauty demands to be noticed; it speaks to us directly like the voice of an intimate friend. If there are people who are indifferent to beauty, then it is surely because they do not perceive it."

-Roger Scruton

Beauty

It's so true, words don't do it justice

So undeniable, it escapes judgment

So obvious that it's redundant

It's so perfect, that it's wondrous

It's the very first gaze at your newborn

It's finally witnessing your gift perform

It's so worth it that you transform

Just to feel worthy of it life-long

It's without flaw and always pure

So honorable, it's almost demure

So effortless but far from obscure

The most admirable thing, and for it you endure

Beauty stands absent of all defect

It unashamedly denounces all precepts

Beauty is absolute perfection to its beholder

A boastful work of art by its molder

"Whatever you do, you need courage. Whatever course you decide upon, there is always someone to tell you that you are wrong. There are always difficulties arising that tempt you to believe your critics are right. To map out a course of action and follow it to an end requires some of the same courage that a soldier needs. Peace has its victories, but it takes brave men and women to win them."

-Ralph Waldo Emerson

Courage

Often times, you only know what you've seen

As it stands, you're only privy to what's gleaned

And if no one ever told you, well then, you're ignorant

And having never experienced, a social misfit

What happens when what you dream about is a foreign thought?

A conceptual truth of something never taught

What if everything you craved and all that's inside of you

Stood in complete conflict with the world around you?

Will you stand in the middle, where the two paths intersect?

A past that is guaranteed and a future you can't dissect.

Will you go and chase after the life you're born to live?

Or build an identity around only what others could give

What you're made of inside are the makings of you

Fulfillment made impossible when you deny the inner truth

So what if your pursuit unleashes the uncertainties of life

What good is our strength, anyhow, without a little strife?

"The key to contentment is to consider. Consider who you are and be satisfied with that. Consider what you have and be satisfied with that. Consider what God's doing and be satisfied with that. You will be amazed at how much more comfortable you'll feel with yourself. Finally, consider this: If contentment cannot be found within yourself, you'll never find it."

-Luci Swindoll

Contentment

It's not that I don't want more than what I already have

To say I don't envy would be a lie on my behalf

The perpetual "upgrading" of life can make you covet

Incapable of living beneath when everyone else is above it

It's not a matter of humility, which some may argue

But personal ownership of the process concerning you

It is a matter of staying in one's own lane

The wisdom to understand that no two men are the same

And if we're all different, from our pasts to our purposes

Then it is unfair to compare in all earnestness

The algorithms of life, varying from person to person

Will always leave you with no comparison

It is futile, then, to diminish your worth

Because of the perceived width of the next person's girth

Your process of development is unilaterally your's

An injustice to your peace to think it anything more

"A man without decision of character can never be said to belong to himself . . . . He belongs to whatever can make captive of him."

-John Foster

Discipline

Sometimes it's not about your ability to do it

For all that glitters isn't gold, and what you see not what you get

Sometimes you have to recognize a bad decision from afar

Curb a bad habit before it leaves a scar

Anything in excess is said to be unhealthy

What was once a small vice is now a gateway

To be unsure and boundless of our margins and limits

Is to unknowingly become our biggest hindrance

An ambiguous identity stems from undisciplined nature

What you will or won't do is impossible to ensure

Your DO's and DON'Ts, your YES's and NO's

Are designed to bring clarity to the person you want to know

Consistency is birthed from a disciplined mind

Purpose springs forth from the cluttered place that it hides

For who you are is understood by your choice of actions

And what you're meant to do revealed from your innate dedications

"Forgiving does not erase the bitter past. A healed memory is not a deleted memory. Instead, forgiving what we cannot forget creates a new way to remember. We change the memory of our past into a hope for our future."

- Louis B. Smedes

Forgiveness

It tops the list as the hardest thing to ascertain

Its absence the beginning link to the longest chain

It is the sweetest thing and the most begrudging pain

The only remover of the darkest stain

Forgiveness appears free, but it's costlier than diamonds

Its price only payable by committed, freed minds

It will cost your life if you choose to live without it

Easier to exercise vengeance than to selflessly remit

Forgiveness is the decided choice to be happy

To rid yourself of negativity that could be

Choosing to forgive is not for its recipient, but you

It is mentally conquering the old to make room for what's new

Forgiveness is life, liberty, and the pursuit of happiness

A personal commitment to never regress

It dissipates a slew of negative reactions

Saving you from the influence of negative factions

"But I think my mistakes became the chemistry for my miracles. I think that my tests became my testimonies."

-T. D. Jakes

Miracles

I forgot to do my assignment, but my teacher didn't show
I just found myself, whom I lost long ago
I felt excruciating pain for years, then it just went away
My harvest came in, after all the times that I'd prayed

Whether small wins or great victories, minor reliefs or huge breaks,
Miracles serve as testaments to our existing faith
They are those things you can't explain, just thankful they happened
Sometimes too customized for words to mention

Miracles are proof –positive that Creator is rooting for you
That you're supported and cared about in everything you do
They are sweet reminders that someone is listening to you
And that you are never alone during your life's pursuits

What's miraculous to you could be normal to the next
But be grateful that you received the answer to your test
Be expectant always, because miracles do happen
And often come better than you could ask or imagine.

"Reputation is an interpretation, more or less accurate, of character."

-Austin O'Malley

Reputation

Don't be concerned about what others say of you

But instead, consider what your behavior ensues

Don't lose sleep or be bothered with others' perceptions

But be mindful, however, of drawn conclusions

Consider your actions as your representative

They precede your entry and are always relative

Be thoughtful of your words, the most timeless displays

They tend to last a lifetime, to our dismay

Protect your name, it goes with you everywhere

Assumptions are waiting with traps that ensnare

Let your definition of self be true to your cause

So that your heart and intent are never camouflaged

Though many will get it wrong and not understand

Allow the company you keep to reflect your hand

And the time you spend to convey your plan

All you have, after all, is what you demand

"Your success and happiness lies in you. Resolve to keep happy, and your joy and you shall form an invincible host against difficulties. "

-Helen Keller

Joy

It's raining outside, but I'll smile anyway

I didn't want it, but it won't ruin my day

And though my feelings were hurt by what you had to say

I won't cry about it, and I'll be okay

Many unfortunate events have happened to me

A cloud of disdain as far as eye can see

I'll wake up determined anyhow and refuse to retreat

I'm encouraged none-the-less and won't compromise my beliefs

My goals seem out of reach and impossible to grasp

But no worries, my hope is going nowhere fast

I chase after my dreams like a hungry lion

An insatiable predator to which I am likened

I will not be deterred and can't be discouraged

Fuel to the fire is an obstacle interpreted

My spirit won't waver and my joy will withstand

I won't be disheartened by defective plans

"Most of what makes a book 'good' is that we are reading it at the right moment for us."

- Alain de Botton

Timing

We often work hard, putting in the tears and the sweat
Committed to the goal, despite perceived threats
We toil and we pray and we cry and we hope
And after what we think is too long, can no longer cope

We study and we train and we just can't understand
How we somehow got stuck with an unlucky hand
We give up the ghost, believing we're not special, after all
Who will keep getting up, fall after all?

So we relinquish the idea that it was ever meant to be
Our whole life we've tried, but opposition won't concede
If it was ever going to happen, it would have by now
Too much of my life now wasted on the prowl

We're forgetting, however, that time reveals all
Our successes, our glory, the reasons for it all
Although desire is there and opportunities plentiful
It is when Time meets Opportunity that we are most capable

"Praise the bridge that carried you over."

-George Colman

Gratitude

When it hurt so badly that I couldn't fathom tomorrow
When I cried so hard I couldn't see past my sorrow
When pain burned so deeply that it challenged all feeling
When disappointment was so pointed, it left me kneeling

When I was forced to push aside and work through it all
When I feigned a smile to disguise my inner walls
When it seemed I didn't have the means to survive
When I was quite content being dead or alive

When I felt so broken to the point of no repair
When I felt suffocated from years of no air
When I cried out for help and produced no rescue
When I was so overwhelmed that I physically couldn't move

I count those moments and times and days to my glory
I commit them to memory for a victorious life story
I celebrate the darkness while I dance in the light
I relish in the fact that I have won every fight

"By justice, a king gives a country stability."

-PROVERBS 29:4

Justice

Nothing has ever felt so right,

There is No darkness too encompassing to combat its light.

Nothing has ever been so absolute,

There is No existing contempt with which to refute.

There is no other hand that can be proven sweeter,

Everyone awaits entry of the greatest leader.

There is nothing in life that is more anticipated,

For upon its arrival, bad is dissipated.

He is fair and righteous and is the hope of every heart,

He is the most beautiful conveyance of speakable art.

He is moral and sound and the embodiment of truth,

He is the purity and determination that exists in only youth.

Without Justice, there is no hope for the future,

Without Justice, the fight for life is not secure.

Without Justice, there is no integrity in doing,

Without Justice, there is no point in pursuing.

I am empowered by Justice, because it lends endless hope.

I am strengthened by Justice, because on its pretenses, I float.

I am encouraged by Justice, because it magnifies what's good.

I am in love with Justice, because He blessed me with motherhood.

PROLOGUE

The deliverance of these words means more than words could ever appropriately express.

For so long, I have gone back and forth, battling the idea of expressing myself in this way, despite others' encouraging. Once I finally accepted the idea, there existed the dilemma of what topic to write about.

All I know, however, is what I've lived to experience and grown to understand. Although these literal pieces of my perspective do not encompass the intimate details of my journey, they successfully highlight the sentiments therein.

It is with overwhelming emotion that I deliver these personal ideals to the world, ideals that were created by from a series of personal experiences. It is with an even greater overflow of feelings that I will forever be able to speak to my son, even in my absence. This ability is made possible through the release of this book—a book that is so much more than compounded words. Rather, it is *my* release, *my* deliverance, and my first step towards *destiny*.

-Chantel K. Demolle

www.ingramcontent.com/pod-product-compliance
Lightning Source LLC
Chambersburg PA
CBHW032137090426
42743CB00007B/624